D1710149

Piece by Piece

Ernestine's Gift for President Roosevelt

Lupe Ruiz-Flores

illustrated by Anna López Real

M Millbrook Press / Minneapolis

For Ernestine Guerrero's daughters: Alice, Charlotte, Mary Helen, and Virginia —L.R.-F.

For A, C, and M who always cheer me on. —A.L.R.

Millbrook Press™
An imprint of Lerner Publishing Group, Inc.
241 First Avenue North
Minneapolis, MN 55401 USA

For reading levels and more information, look up this title at www.lernerbooks.com.

Image credits: Courtesy of the Franklin D. Roosevelt Presidential Library and Museum, Hyde Park, NY, p. 30 (clock case; letters); Courtesy of the Guerrero Family, p. 30 (Ernestine Guerrero photo).

Designed by Viet Chu.
Main body text set in Dante MT Std. Typeface provided by Monotype Typography.
The illustrations in this book were created with graphite and colored pencil on paper.

Library of Congress Cataloging-in-Publication Data

Names: Ruiz-Flores, Lupe, author. | López Real, Anna, illustrator.
Title: Piece by piece : Ernestine's gift for President Roosevelt / Lupe Ruiz-Flores ; illustrated by Anna López Real.
Other titles: Ernestine's gift for President Roosevelt
Description: Minneapolis : Millbrook Press, [2023] | Includes bibliographical references. | Audience: Ages 5–9 | Audience: Grades 2–3 | Summary: "During the Great Depression, Ernestine Guerrero's family didn't have much. The true story of a resourceful Mexican American teen who made a remarkable gift to thank President Roosevelt for the food aid that helped them survive!" —Provided by publisher.
Identifiers: LCCN 2022056367 (print) | LCCN 2022056368 (ebook) | ISBN 9781728460437 (lib. bdg.) | ISBN 9798765602072 (ebook) | ISBN 9798765602041 (epub)
Subjects: LCSH: Guerrero, Ernestine, 1915–1956—Juvenile literature. | Mexican American teenage girls—Texas—San Antonio—Juvenile literature. | Mexican Americans—Texas—San Antonio—Juvenile literature. | Roosevelt, Franklin D. (Franklin Delano), 1882–1945—Juvenile literature. | New Deal, 1933–1939—Texas—Juvenile literature. | San Antonio (Tex.)—Economic conditions—20th century—Juvenile literature. | United States—Economic conditions—1918–1945—Juvenile literature. | Wood-carving—Juvenile literature.
Classification: LCC F394.S2119 M51742 2023 (print) | LCC F394.S2119 (ebook) | DDC 973.917—dc23/eng/20221125

LC record available at https://lccn.loc.gov/2022056367
LC ebook record available at https://lccn.loc.gov/2022056368

Manufactured in the United States of America
1-51510-50382-1/27/2023

If you look closely, treasure can be found in unexpected places.

Just ask Ernestine Guerrero, the second oldest
in a family of six children. She was only fourteen
in 1929 when the Great Depression
destroyed the American economy,
including her hometown of San Antonio, Texas.

Before the Great Depression began,
Ernestine had worked together with her father, a carpenter.
Because her father couldn't afford to hire a helper,
Ernestine had dropped out of school
when she was nine years old
to become his assistant.

She carried the lighter tools.
Piece by piece, she spread glue on each portion
of wallpaper that was to be hung.
She stirred the paint in the cans
and used a small hammer to drive nails into wood.

They rode to work every day in their Model T truck,
driving from job to job across the city.

But now her father was unemployed
and so was she.

Thanks to the Great Depression,
prices for crops and livestock fell,
and farmers couldn't make enough money.

When they couldn't pay their bills,
they had to abandon their land.

Banks closed.
Millions of people lost their jobs,
their homes, and their life savings.

Not just in the United States but in countries everywhere.
Piece by piece, the world as they knew it fell apart.

Ernestine's father could no longer find work as a carpenter.
His customers couldn't afford to pay him.
With no money,
Ernestine's family had no choice but to join the long breadlines
of desperate, hungry people
waiting for free food from the government.

When they got to the front of the line,
sometimes they would get a sugar pine wood crate
filled with groceries.
Other times the food supplies would run out,
and they would go home empty-handed.

Ernestine knew that her family,
like so many others,
would not survive without
President Franklin D. Roosevelt's
New Deal program,
which provided opportunities for jobs,
help for the farmers, and hope
for the nation—as well as those crates of free food.

The president needed to know that his programs
were really helping families like hers
to stay alive during these hard times.

Ernestine was convinced that if he understood
how grateful they were,
the food relief would continue
for as long as they needed it.

Since she had no money to buy him a thank-you gift,
Ernestine would make one.
But what could a poor girl from Texas
possibly make for the president of the United States?

One day, her uncle
gave her a woodworking pattern for a clock case
called the Chimes of Normandy.

Ernestine studied it closely
    and discovered the pattern required 156 pieces of wood.
        Each piece had to fit together
            to make the 40-inch-high clock case.

It seemed like an impossible task,
and that's how she knew it was the right way to thank the president.
He had done the impossible in saving her family from starvation,
so it was only right that she give him an impossible gift right back.

She knew it would be the hardest thing
she had ever done.

She would take her time
to make it fit for a president
whom she greatly admired.

But where would she get the wood?
Wood cost money.

Ernestine's father pointed to the empty
food-relief crates piled up in the backyard,
crates that had once held free bags of flour and beans.
"Why don't you build something pretty
out of those boxes for him?"

Was he joking?

Carve intricate designs out of dirty crates for President Roosevelt?

Hmm . . . maybe . . .

There were plenty of containers in the backyard.
And she missed working with wood.

So Ernestine spent days removing the nails from each empty box.
She needed to improve her skills
before she could make the real thing,
so piece by piece, she practiced
on wood from the food crates.

She used a coping saw for cutting out shapes.
Carved hollows and curves into the wood with a gouge.
Chiseled out lines and cleaned up flat surfaces.

At first, she made a lot of mistakes.
But she was determined to make it work.
Her gift had to be just right for the president.

And after a year of practice, it was.

She spent the next year cutting the pattern and carving the interlaced decorative designs with a coping saw.

Then Ernestine applied stain,
piece by piece,
until each one gleamed.

Next, she glued all 156 pieces
of wood together.

The final part was the clock itself.
There was no money to buy one,
but that didn't stop Ernestine.
She carved a fake one out of wood.
It wouldn't really keep time, but it would have to do.

But now . . .

The three tower spires had no bells.
Her heart sank.
There was no money to spare.

Yet somehow her father came up with a few pennies, sacrificing what little they had.

She bought three tiny parakeet cage bells and placed them in the towers.

With only a third-grade education,
Ernestine struggled to write a letter
to accompany her gift to the president
expressing her gratitude
for all that he had done for her family and the nation.

She worked and worked and worked on the letter.
She erased words over and over again.
She checked the spelling.
Finally, the letter was ready.

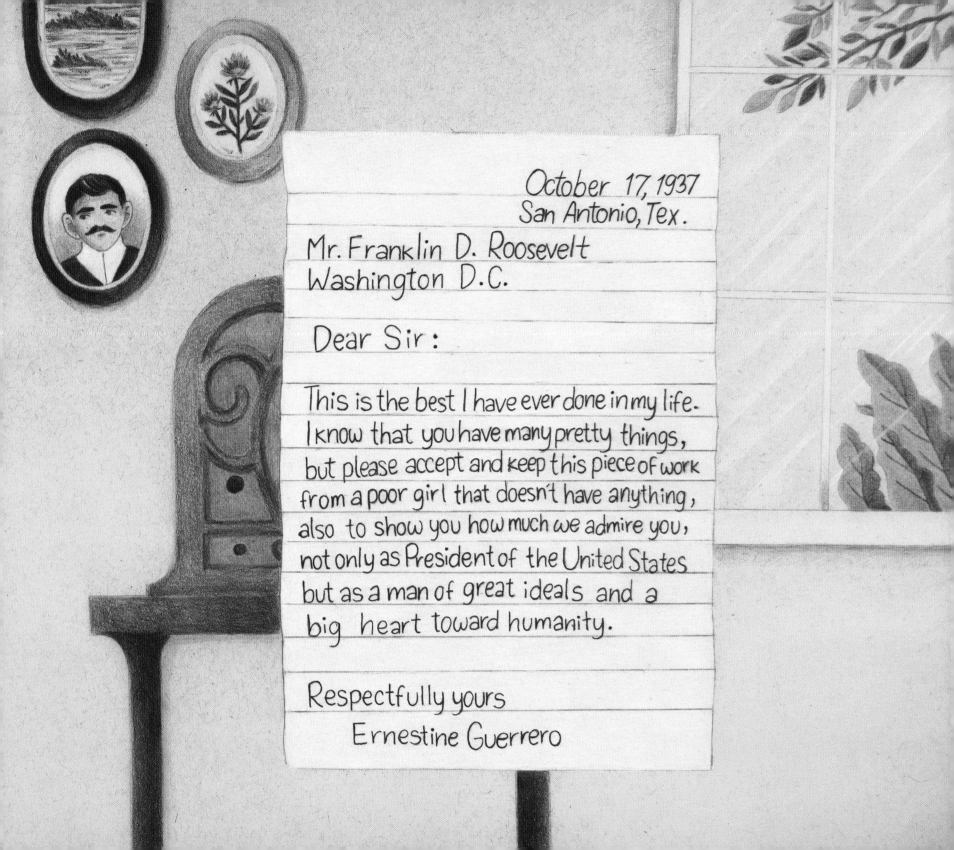

On October 17, 1937, Ernestine and her father went to the post office.
At last, the clock case was on its way to the White House.

Days passed.
Then weeks.
Ernestine worried.
Had the president received the clock case?
Did he like it?

She waited
and waited
and waited.
She checked for mail every day.

And then . . .
A letter of thanks arrived.
It was signed by President Franklin D. Roosevelt himself.

He was impressed!
Ernestine's hard work had paid off.
Her gift of gratitude had made the president
understand that his New Deal program was working.

A few years later, Ernestine's clock case traveled once more.
This time from the White House to the
Franklin D. Roosevelt Library and Museum
in Hyde Park, New York,
where it, along with her letter, is still on display today.

Every year, millions of visitors come through
and admire the woodwork of Ernestine Guerrero,
the girl who, piece by piece,
created a gift fit for a president
and showed us all that
if you look closely,
treasure can be found
in unexpected places.

Ernestine Guerrero
The Chimes of
Normandy   1937

Author's Note

Ernestine Guerrero as an adult, date unknown

This book was inspired by a February 26, 2017, article by Paula Allen titled "San Antonio Teen's Gift Impressed FDR," which I read in my local newspaper, the *San Antonio Express-News*. I began researching Ernestine Guerrero and was able to locate one of her relatives, which led to an interview with her four daughters.

The clock case is named after cathedral bells in the Normandy region of France. The sculpture and Ernestine's letter to the president are part of an exhibit at the Franklin D. Roosevelt Presidential Library and Museum in upstate New York. Unfortunately, the letter from the president thanking Ernestine for the gift was destroyed in a house fire.

Ernestine Guerrero was a Mexican American girl born in Temple, Texas, in 1915. She loved to play basketball and was nicknamed Tina Bucket because she made so many baskets while playing on a women's team.

After completing the clock case for President Roosevelt, Ernestine got a job working at a San Antonio dry cleaner. It's unknown whether she kept up her woodworking hobby. She married in 1939 and raised four daughters. She did not ever speak of the clock case to her children, and they learned about its existence only many years after her 1956 death. Ernestine never knew that she had become part of history when her two-year labor of love created from discarded wooden crates became a permanent display in the FDR museum. Her daughters have visited the display in New York and are extremely proud that their mother's memory is being kept alive.

The author wishes to thank the Library of Congress, the Franklin D. Roosevelt Presidential Library and Museum, and *San Antonio Express-News* columnist Paula Allen for their help in researching this story.

The author also thanks Ernestine Guerrero's four daughters, Alice, Charlotte, Mary Helen, and Virginia, for their interview about their mother. The author is grateful to editors Carol Hinz and Leila Sales of Millbrook Press for believing in this story. Additional thanks to Daniel Morales for consulting on the depictions of woodworking. Thanks also to Anna López Real for her beautiful illustrations. And a special thank-you to the Society of Children's Book Writers and Illustrators.

Ernestine's completed *Chimes of Normandy* clock case

The full letter Ernestine Guerrero sent to President Roosevelt along with the clock case.

Glossary

breadline: a line of people waiting to receive free food

chisel: a tool with a straight cutting edge that's used for drawing lines and cleaning up flat surfaces

coping saw: a handsaw used to cut intricate external shapes and interior cutouts in woodworking or carpentry

food relief: food given directly from the government to people in need

Franklin Delano Roosevelt (January 30, 1882–April 12, 1945): the thirty-second president of the United States, known as FDR. He was the only US president to be elected four times. He led the country through much of the Great Depression and World War II (1939–1945).

gouge: a tool with a curved cutting edge used in a variety of forms and sizes for carving hollows, rounds, and sweeping curves

Great Depression: an economic collapse that began in the United States on October 29, 1929. Millions of people were out of work. Construction in many cities stopped. Farmers' crop prices fell. Ordinary citizens suffered when they lost their homes. Many people had no money to buy food. This depression lasted more than a decade and affected other countries around the world as well.

New Deal: President Franklin D. Roosevelt's New Deal programs reduced poverty, cut unemployment, and created improvements in industry, agriculture, finance, waterpower, labor, and housing. These programs gave the American people jobs and hope.

Source Notes

"Why don't you . . . boxes for him": Ernestine Guerrero, letter to Franklin D. Roosevelt, October 17, 1937, National Archives, https://fdr.artifacts.archives.gov/objects/29347/the-chimes-of-normandy.

"Dear Sir . . . Respectfully yours, Ernestine Guerrero": Guerrero, letter to Franklin D. Roosevelt.

Selected Bibliography

Allen, Paula. "San Antonio Teen's Gift Impressed FDR." *San Antonio Express-News*, February 26, 2017.

"The Chimes of Normandy, 1937." Franklin D. Roosevelt Presidential Library. Accessed November 27, 2022. https://fdrlibrary.tumblr.com/post/51912686884/day-29-june-1-the-chimes-of-normandy-1937.

Cohen, Robert, and Eleanor Roosevelt. *Dear Mrs. Roosevelt: Letters from Children of the Great Depression.* Chapel Hill, NC: University of North Carolina Press, 2002.

De Young, C. Coco. *A Letter to Mrs. Roosevelt.* New York: Delacorte, 1999.

"Franklin D. Roosevelt." The White House. Accessed November 27, 2022. https://www.whitehouse.gov/1600/Presidents/franklindroosevelt.

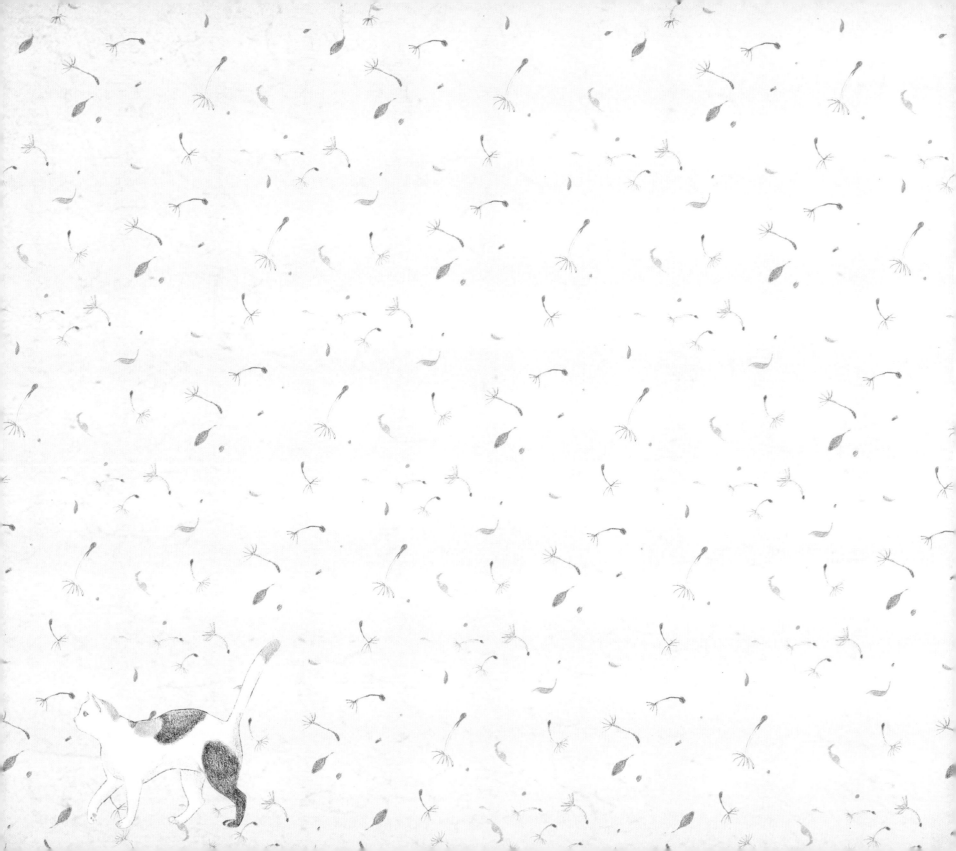